THE WIZARD'S

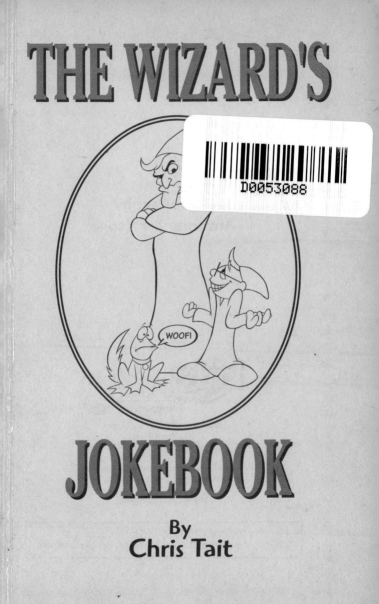

WOOF!

JOKEBOOK

By
Chris Tait

Cover art by
Anthony J. Falcone

Incorporated

Copyright © 2001 Kidsbooks, Inc.
230 Fifth Avenue
New York, NY 10001

Visit us at www.kidsbooks.com.
Volume discounts available for group purchases.

What does a wizard's cat like just before it goes to bed?

A sorcerer of milk!

★ ☽ ★

Why are wizards so good in fishing school?

Because they really know how to cast a spell!

★★★

What do math wizards say when they lift a curse?

Hex-a-gone!

What did the wizard say when he couldn't find his wife?

Witch way did she go?

★★★

What did the witch say to the monster who ate too fast?

Wow, you really are a goblin!

★☾★

If three ghosts conjured by a wizard run a race, who will win?

The one with the most spirit!

★★★

What did the wizard say when he met the witch he was going to marry?

So, this is the bride and broom!

★☾★

What does the wizard's sister eat when she goes to the beach?

Sand-witches!

What is the favorite name for
werewolves?

Harry!

★★★

When the wizard found his friend,
what had she been doing?

Witchhiking!

★☽★

What did the wizard tell his wife after
he tried to change her into a bird?

I've got some bat news . . . !

★★★

What is the wizard's favorite soap
opera called?

All My Cauldrons!

How does a wizard keep his potions safe from burglars?

With a warlock!

★☾★

Where do wizards go to test their skill?

Spelling bees!

★★★

What does a wizard say when he wants the lights to go on?

Abra candelabra!

★☾★

What did the wizard's wife say when he changed her into a bird?

Owl fly away!

What did the wizard name his daughter?
Wand-a!

★★★

What do you call a wizard who tells the weather?
A forecaster!

★☽★

Why do wizards need housekeepers?
To take care of the magic dust!

★★★

Why did the witch's children do so well in school?
Because they were wiz kids!

★☽★

What do you call a phony wizard?
A magi-sham!

★★★

What do you call a wizard with basic good manners?
Simply charming!

What did the little wizard say when his first spell worked?

Hexellent!

★ ☽ ★

Are all wizards good?

Not hex-actly!

★★★

What do the young wizards call their oldest teacher?

Tyrannosaurus Hex!

★ ☽ ★

Why don't single wizards dance?

Because they don't have ghoul-friends!

★★★

What did the little wizards call their baseball team?

The Bat News Bears!

What's a wizard's favorite subject in school?

Spelling!

★★★

Why didn't the wizard predict the future for a living?

There was no prophet in it!

★☽★

What did the wizard say to his favorite bird?

Owl see ya later!

How many wizards does it take to change a lightbulb?

None. Wizards don't need to use lightbulbs!

★☽★

What kind of jewelry do wizards wear?
Charm bracelets!

★★★

Where do young wizards go to learn?

Charm school!

★☽★

What do little witches call art day at school?

Witch craft day!

★★★

What was wrong with the forgetful wizard's memory?

It had a tendency to wand-er!

What did the wizard say to his girl-friend before the dance?

My dear, you look wand-erful!

★★★

What dance did the wizard take the witch to?

The Crystal Ball!

★☽★

What did the wizard say to the vampire when he knew he was wrong?

Sorry, it was a mis-stake!

★★★

Why did the wizard send his friend an hourglass in the mail?

He wanted to see time travel!

★☽★

What did the wizard's friend say after he turned him into an antelope?

That's gnus to me!

How do witches know how much money you have?

Because they know how to tell your fortune!

★ ☽ ★

Why do wizards love to eat at family restaurants?

Because they have the biggest potions!

★ ★ ★

Why don't wizards like to cast spells on boats?

They get potion sickness!

Why was the little wizard angry at his big sister?

Because, she was always potion him around!

★ ☽ ★

What did the old wizard say to his frustrated pupil?

Stay calm, my son, potions is a virtue!

★★★

What do wizards use to open haunted houses?

A spooo-key!

★ ☽ ★

Why don't wizards need glasses?

Because they have eye of newt!

★★★

Why are ghosts vegetarians?

Because it's cruel to haunt animals!

What did the wizard say to the spirit of the gambling man?

You don't have a ghost of a chance!

★★★

How do wizards guarantee peace?

They get a warlock!

★☽★

What do little warlocks love on their nachos?

Cheese wiz!

★★★

Who is the most famous wiz of all?

Oz just about to ask you that!

What do wizards call phony spells?

Hocus bogus!

★★★

What did the wizard say after the fishing accident?

Help! Hook-has poke-us!

★☽★

What do wizards say to their young students who can't concentrate?

Hocus focus!

★★★

What do you say to a wizard who is a daydreamer?

Wish not, wand not!

★☽★

What does a wizard say when he gets to his front door?

Open says me!

What did the wizard say to the little girl who wanted to study magic?

Witching you the best of luck!

★★★

What did the wizard think of the story about the little, flying people?

It was fairy interesting!

★☾★

What did the wizard say after he lost a game of chess to the little sprite?

Fairy 'nuff!

★★★

What did the wizard say to the lazy monster?

Quit dragon your tail!

★☾★

Where did the wizard meet his elf friend for their fishing trip?

Down by the dwarf!

What did the wizard say when his little sidekick went away on vacation?

I feel so elfless!

★☽★

Why can't babies do magic?

Because they don't know how to spell!

★★★

What did the wizard say when he was buying the elf's prize walking stick?

Gnome your price!

★☽★

What do American fairies sing at the beginning of every baseball game?

Stars and Sprites!

Why do wizards make good friends?
Because they're charming!

★★★

How are wizards' books held together?
They're spellbound!

★ ☾ ★

What do wizards call their magic books?
The Go-spell!

★★★

What is it called when wizards get together and sing without instruments?
Acca-spell-a!

★ ☾ ★

What is the name of the richest American wizard?
Rocka-spell-a!

★★★

What did the elf say when he was tired of Oz?

There's no place like gnome!

Why do witches chew gum?

Because they're afraid of having bat breath!

★☽★

What do speedy monsters love to do most?

Dragon racing!

★★★

Why did the witch decide to get a new broom?

She wanted to make a clean sweep of it!

★☽★

Why did the witch need to practice with her new broom?

Because she needed to brush up on her flying!

★★★

Why do witches fly to their secret caves?

Because it's too far to walk!

What did the wizard's kitten say
before his magic trick?

> *Abra cat-abra!*

★★★

What did the pirate want the witch
to find for him?

> *Sleeping booty!*

★☾★

Where do witches go when they run
out of eye of newt and tongue of frog?

> *To the gross-ery store!*

"Knock, knock!"
"Who's there?"
"Witch!"
"Witch who?"

> *"Witches to put a spell on you!"*

"Knock, knock!"
"Who's there?"
"Wiz!"
"Wiz who?"

"Wiz a matter, you don't recognize me?"

★☽★

If you spin around and around, what kind of magic will you create?

A dizzy spell!

★★★

What kind of spell makes you thirsty?

A dry spell!

★☽★

"Knock, knock!"
"Who's there?"
"Ghost!"
"Ghost who?"

"Ghost to show, nobody remembers my name!"

"Knock, knock!"

"Who's there?"

"Boo!"

"Boo who?"

"Hey, don't cry, I'm a friendly ghost!"

★★★

What is a witch's favorite pet?

A wart hog!

★ ☾ ★

Why are magicians such fast readers?

*Because they know how to wiz
through a good book!*

★★★

"Knock, knock!"

"Who's there?"

"Gnome!"

"Gnome who?"

*"Gnome 'atter how many times I
knock, you won't let me in!"*

What did the wizard say to the reptile that surprised him?

Hey you, don't snake up on me!

★☽★

What is a wizard's favorite drink?

Witches' brew!

★★★

What is the spell for keeping animals indoors?

Z-O-O!

★☽★

Other than garlic, what is a vampire's least favorite food?

Stake!

Why don't vampires change into pelicans?

Because pelicans are too big to fly in through bedroom windows!

★☽★

What is a vampire's favorite sport?

Batsball!

★★★

"Knock, knock!"
"Who's there?"
"Bats!"
"Bats who?"
"Bats a matter, don't you recognize me?"

★☽★

Who is a witch's favorite musician?

Bats Domino!

★★★

How do wizards roast their marshmallows?

With dragon's breath!

What is a wizard's favorite cereal?

Lucky Charms!

★★★

What do you call the most powerful wizard of all?

Whatever he wants you to!

★☽★

What do you call a female wizard at the beach?

A sandy-witch!

★★★

What do you call a criminal elf?

A lepre-con!

★☽★

What do you call a leprechaun's dog?

A four-leafed Rover!

What do Eskimo leprechaun's ke at the end of the rainbow?

A lucky pot of cold!

★★★

What did the Bigfoot put in his gard

Sas-squash!

★☽★

What do you call a sloppy magic creature in a pond?

The Loch Mess monster!

★★★

What did the umpire say when the wizard was up to bat?

Swing and a miss-tical!

★☽★

"Knock, knock!"
"Who's there?"
"Who!"
"Who who?"
"Hey, you must be the wizard

What do wizards wear when they get out of the bath?

Their magic robes!

★ ☽ ★

What did the wizard say when he had the television remote?

Press-to chango!

★★★

How did the wizard catch the big fish?

Tricka trout!

★ ☽ ★

What color robe does the wizard's cat wear?

Purr-ple, of course!

★★★

What do you call an elf with a green thumb?

A garden gnome!

What kind of seafood do gnomes like best?

Sh-elf fish!

★ ☽ ★

What kind of monsters spit the most?

Gob-lins!

★★★

What kind of candy do goblins hate the most?

Gob-stoppers!

★ ☽ ★

What do you find in a monster's belly button?

Gob-lint!

★★★

What do fairies love to drink?

Sprite!

★ ☽ ★

What does a wizard call a naughty child?

A brat-cadabra!

Where do wizards go for cold medicine?

To witch doctors!

★★★

What is a gnome's favorite singer?

Elf-is Presley!

★☽★

What did the wizard call his little friend who thought only of himself?

S-elf ish!

★★★

When the student turned a dog into a cat, what did the wizard say?

Con-cat-ulations! Hexellent job!

★☽★

What sound do witches make when they start their transportation?

Brrrrroooooom, brrrrroooooooom, brrrrooooom!

Why did the wizard turn himself into
a skeleton?

> Because his wife was getting under
> his skin!

★☽★

What did she call him when she saw
what he had done?

> Gutless!

★★★

What did the wizard think of having bats
that could bite hanging from his roof?

> He thought it was fang-tastic!

★☽★

What did the wizard say when he
met the ghost?

> Well, good evening, sir. How do
> you boo?

★★★

Why do dragons sleep all day?

> So they can get out at knights!

What kind of teams did the monsters want when playing baseball?

Ghouls versus boys!

★★★

What did the surfer think after the wizard changed him into a frog?

He thought it was toad-ally awesome!

★☽★

Why did the wizard think the vampire had a cold?

Because of all the coffin!

What did the witch offer guests who stayed at her house?

Broom and board!

★★★

What did the ghouls make their loudest member?

Their spooksman!

★☽★

What do witches like to give little children for dessert?

Eye scream!

★★★

Why was the wizard so excited to get his new spiders home?

He wanted to take them out for a spin!

★☽★

Why was the wizard upset to learn that his spiders were already married?

Because he hadn't been invited to the webbing!

What did the spider say to the fly in the wizard's castle?

Welcome to my Web site!

★★★

What did the fly call the spider's lair?

A lethal webbin'!

★☾★

What did the witch need when her sewing machine got broken?

A spin doctor!

Why did the wizard tell the ghost to go to a pep rally?

> *To get some school spirit!*

★☽★

How did the eight-legged creature know that he had met his true love?

> *He just spider!*

★★★

What did the wizard say to the vain troll?

> *Oh, get ogre yourself!*

★☽★

What did the three ogres who lived under the wizard's bridge want to install?

> *A troll booth!*

★★★

What do San Francisco ogres like better than the bus?

> *The troll-ey car!*

What did the little wizard say when his father asked him why he wanted a lizard?

Because I guana!

★★★

What did the wizard say to the vampire while it was still in its coffin?

Now listen, I don't want you to flip your lid!

★☽★

What did the sick ghost say to the wizard when it got out of the hospital?

So, do you want to hear about my apparition?

★★★

Why did the wizard call the ghost a phony?

Because he could see right through him!

What did the wizard use to open the tomb?

A skeleton key!

★ ☽ ★

What did the wizard call the foreign ghost?

An imported spirit!

★★★

When the ghost moved, what did it tell the wizard it would miss?

All of its possessions!

★ ☽ ★

What did the wizard sing to the cowboy elf?

"Gnome on the Range"!

★★★

Why was the skeleton lonely?

Because he had no body to see!

★ ☽ ★

What do you call bird ghosts?

Sea-ghouls!

★★★

What did the wizard call the skeleton's head?

Numbskull!

★☽★

Why couldn't the witch fly?

She was broom-sick!

★★★

What did she do about it?

She took the broom temperature!

When the student got a wand, what did the wizard say?

Why don't you try it out for a spell?

★★★

Why did the wizard shrink his wife down to a tiny size?

Because he wanted a wrist-witch!

★☽★

Why did the witch think her broom was so fast?

It had 300-hearse power!

★★★

Why do witches like shopping so much?

Because they love to hag-gle!

★☽★

What did the wizard call his candle-making wife?

The wick-ed witch!

What did the wizard tell the student to do after dinner?

His gnomework!

★★★

What did the wizard call the birds that haunted his backyard?

Polter-geese!

★☽★

What did the wizard say he needed after he spilled food on his outfit?

Soap on a robe!

What did he sing while he washed his outfit?

Robe-a-dub-dub!

★ ☽ ★

What do wizards love to give their spiders to eat?

Corn on the cobweb!

★★★

What was the witch's cat supposed to catch?

The gingerbread mouse!

★ ☽ ★

What was the wizards' meeting group called?

Conjured citizens!

★★★

What did the wizard say to his daughter before the big test?

Good luck on the hex-am!

What happened when she was caught cheating?

She was ex-spelled!

★ ☽ ★

Who helps the witch doctor?

The curse nurse!

★★★

How did the wizard's horse do at the races?

She came in cursed place!

★ ☽ ★

What did the wizard come up with in the lab?

A brand-new hex-periment!

41

What did the wizard do to get rid of termites?

He had them hex-terminated!

★🌙★

How did the wizard's wife feel after she got fleas?

W-itchy!

★★★

What was the wizard's daughter named in the beauty pageant?

Miss Tic (Mystic)!

★🌙★

How did the wizard find the ingredients he needed for his spell?

With a toad map!

★★★

How did the wizard feel after he heard the creepy music?

Ear-ee!

What did the trees say after the ghost went through their leaves?

Well, shiver me timbers!

★ ☽ ★

What kind of animal does a ghost knight ride?

A haunted horse!

★★★

Where do wizards get their soup from?

In can tations!

★ ☽ ★

What do you call a dancing spirit?

The boogie man!

★★★

What do you call a tent for the undead?

A cree-pee!

★ ☽ ★

What do ghosts see in the rainbow?

A whole specter of colors!

How did the wizard get to his house when the drawbridge was broken?

With a rowmoat!

★ ☾ ★

What did the wizard ask his art class to do?

Draw-bridge!

★★★

What did the wizard get while he was rowing in his moat?

Moat-shun sickness!

★ ☾ ★

Where did the haunted suit of armor go for classes?

Knight school!

★★★

What did the wizard call the knight who loved to joust?

Lance-a-lot!

Why couldn't the knight go riding?

Because he had a horse throat!

★★★

When the wizard tried to go riding, what did the horse say?

Hoof got to be kidding!

★ ☽ ★

Why did the wizard get wet when he was riding?

Because it was reining!

★★★

What do you call the wizard's unhappy feeling after riding the horse?

Sad-dle!

★ ☽ ★

What did the wizard say to stop the knight from fighting?

Joust a moment!

What did the wizard say about the word *knight*?

> *It had a duel meaning!*

★ ☽ ★

What did the wizard make the knight do?

> *He made him sword on his life to stop fighting!*

★★★

What did the knight give his horse after a wedding?

> *A bridle sweet!*

What did the knight do as he rode his horse along a riverbank?

He went trot fishing!

★ ☽ ★

What was the favorite fruit of the wizard's horse?

Canter-lope!

★★★

What did the wizard call the knight who made lunch as he was riding?

The galloping gourmet!

★ ☽ ★

What did the wizard's wife say when she wanted to be covered in gold?

Alchem-me!

★★★

What did the wizard give his wife to make her feel better?

An elix-her!

What did the wizard call the princess who woke up angry from her long slumber?

Slapping beauty!

★ ☽ ★

What did the wizard give his wife when he wanted to protect her?

A suit of arm-her!

★★★

Who was the favorite knight of the wizard's horse?

Donkey-oatey (Don Quixote)!

★ ☽ ★

How did the wizard clean his dog?

He made sham-poodle!

★★★

What did the wizard want for a scary dog?

A terror-eer (terrier)!

What did the wizard say to his dog after cleaning him?

My, don't you look houndsome!

★★★

What did the witch say when asked if she was sure she didn't want another cat?

I'm paw-sitive!

★☽★

What was the wizard's dog's favorite vegetable?

Collie-flower!

★★★

What did the wizard's dog do after a long run?

It lay down in a poodle of sweat!

★☽★

What kind of dog do zombie's own?

Rot-weilers!

What did the wizard call his dog when it was unhappy?

Melon-collie!

★ ☽ ★

What did the wizard give his cat for Easter?

Chocolate mouse!

★★★

What did the wizard's daughter say after he told her that he had changed her into a cat?

Well, that's mews to me!

What did the wizard's cat say to the mirror?

Don't you look purr-fect?

★★★

How did the wizard give the cat what it wanted?

Easy. He made copy-cats!

★☽★

What did the wizard's cat say when it hurt its paw?

Me-ow!

★★★

What did the wizard say when he saw the cat fly over the castle wall?

Must be the cat-a-pult!

★☽★

What did the wizard's daughter say when her cat was missing?

It's a cat-astrophe!

What did the wizard call the stone felines guarding the entrance to his castle?

Cat-er-pillars!

★★★

What did the rodent say to the wizard?

Mice to meet you!

★☽★

What did the witch call the gloves that she made for her cat?

Kitten mittens!

★★★

Where did the wizard take his wife in the winter?

To the Snow Ball!

★☽★

Why were the fish in the moat so smart?

They were always in a school!

Where did the fish in the moat never want to end up?

In squid row!

★★★

How did the frog get across the moat?

It went for a pike-fish ride!

★☾★

How did the wizard know that he had caught a big fish in his moat?

He could tell by the scales!

★★★

What did the fish say to its friend when a horse fell into the moat?

See horse?

What did the fish in the moat play
after school?

> Trout or dare!

★ ☽ ★

What did the witch say when she fell
into the moat?

> My eels are killing me!

★★★

What did the wizard say when he
heard the mermaids singing?

> Those fish are out of tuna!

★ ☽ ★

What is the wizard's favorite fish
lullaby?

> Salmon-chanted evening!

★★★

What did the wizard call his favorite
snake?

> The Lizard of Oz!

What did the wizard call his hallways after he had snakeskin wallpaper installed?

His rept-aisles!

★★★

What animal does the wizard always say is lying?

The bull frog!

★☽★

Why did the wizard say that you should never warm up to a snake?

Because they're cold-blooded!

★★★

What did the wizard use to warn other drivers that he was coming?

A frog horn!

★☽★

What is the wizard's favorite swamp flower?

The croak-us!

What did the wizard's son say when the wizard started to tell him the reptile joke?

You already toad me that one!

★ ☽ ★

How do frogs get clean?

They use croak on a rope!

★ ★ ★

What did the frog say to his son who was late for school?

Hop to it!

★ ☽ ★

What do you call the wizard who collects wildlife from the swamp?

A toad-hog!

Where did the wizard go to turn the student back into a boy?

The changing room!

★★★

What did the wizard call his smallest fishing rod?

A tad-pole!

★☾★

What did the cat in the wizard's castle have to do?

Mousework!

★★★

What did the wizard say when the cat caught the mouse?

Micely done!

★☾★

What did the wizard's blackbird think about the big party?

Oh, he was raven about it!

Was the wizard's blackbird hungry after the party?

> *He was raven-ous!*

★★★

Why couldn't the cat talk after catching the rodent?

> *He had a mouse-ful!*

★☽★

What did the blackbird say when it took the dinghy across the moat?

> *Crow, crow, crow your boat!*

Why did the wizard's cat want to put rodents in the freezer?

He wanted to see mice cubes!

★ ☽ ★

What did the wizard get when he crossed his hamster with a bodybuilder?

A mouse-el man!

★★★

What did the wizard get when he crossed a rooster with a rabbit?

An ear-ly bird!

★ ☽ ★

What did the wizard get when he crossed a baboon with a tool kit?

A monkey wrench!

★★★

What did the wizard get when he crossed fruit with a math book?

Apple pi!

What did the wizard get when he crossed a liar with the Gouda?

Cheater cheese!

★ ☽ ★

What did the wizard get when he crossed a snake and a symphony?

A boa conductor!

★★★

What did the wizard's frog say to the snake?

Hiss me now or lose me forever!

★ ☽ ★

What was the snake's favorite subject in school?

Hiss-story!

★★★

What did the wizard's snake use to eat?

Fork-chops!

What did the wizard get when he crossed a vine with a snake?

Poison ivy!

★ ☽ ★

What did the wizard say when he cast a spell on his snake?

Abra-da cobra!

★★★

What did the wizard get when he crossed a lizard with the man who cut his grass?

A gardener snake!

What did the wizard get when he crossed a squid with a cat?

An octo-puss!

★ ☽ ★

What did the woman say when the wizard told her how much the spell would cost?

That's a charm and a leg!

★★★

What did the wizard's frog say to the toad?

So, warts on your mind?

★ ☽ ★

What did the wizard get when he crossed a snowball and a snake?

Frostbite!

★★★

What did the wizard get when he crossed a heckler with a parrot?

A mockingbird!

What did the wizard's owl say to the raven?

Sparrow a moment?

★★★

What did the wizard get when he crossed a baseball player and a chicken?

Fowlball!

★☽★

What did the wizard get when he combined a duck and a funny book?

Quackerjokes!

★★★

Where did the wizard get his owl?

The storkmarket!

★☽★

What did the wizard call the bird with an eye patch?

Polly the Pirate!

What did the wizard tell the Cyclops
who was playing baseball?

Keep your eye on the ball!

★ ☾ ★

What did the wizard call it when he
pulled a rabbit out of his hat three
times in a row?

A hat trick!

★★★

What did the witch get when she
combined a circus and a school?

The class clown!

★ ☾ ★

What did the witch get when she
combined tools with a toboggan?

A sled hammer!

★★★

What did the wizard call his spirit
friends from Europe?

Portu-ghosts!

What did the suit of armor miss about being worn?

The knight life!

★★★

What did the suit of armor say after being left out in the rain?

I think I'll just lie down for a rust!

★ ☽ ★

How did the ghost feel after walking all the way home to the castle?

He was dead on his feet!

★★★

What did the wizard feed the Italian ghost?

Spook-ghetti!

What did the wizard call the story that the knight told about his horse?

A pony-tail!

★ ☽ ★

What did the wizard get when he crossed a cola with a bike?

A pop-cycle!

★★★

What did the wizard get when he crossed a frog and a bunny?

A ribbit rabbit!

★ ☽ ★

What do witches use in their hair?

Scare-spray!

★★★

What did the zombie tell the wizard?

I'm rotten to my friends!

★ ☽ ★

What did the wizard call the knight after his clothes shrank?

Tight in shining armor!

★★★

What did the wizard call the zombie's hair?

Mouldy locks!

★☽★

What did the witch call the movie she was making about the midnight hour?

A dark-umentary!

★★★

What did the witch call her popular recipe book?

A best-smeller!

★☽★

What did the wizard get when he combined a hyena with a banana?

Peels of laughter!

Where did the wizard's daughter find her first boyfriend?

At the Meet Ball!

★ ☽ ★

Why did the wizard tell the joke to the ice?

He wanted to see if he could crack it up!

★★★

What did the wizard get when he crossed a scientist and a duck?

A wise quacker!

★ ☽ ★

Why was the wizard trying to make a legless cow?

To get ground beef!

★★★

What did the wizard get when he crossed a goat and an owl?

A hoot 'n' nanny!

What did the wizard get when he crossed a whale with candy?

Blubber gum!

★★★

What did the witch eat for breakfast?

Dreaded wheat!

★☽★

What did the wizard get when he crossed a cow with a nap?

A bulldozer!

How much did the wizard tell the pirate it would be to get his ears pierced?

A buck an ear (buccaneer)!

★ ☽ ★

What did the wizard get when he crossed the toad and the lizard?

A croakadile!

★★★

Where do ghosts go swimming?

In the Dead Sea!

What kind of food do elves like to make?

Shortbread!

★★★

What did the wizard get when he crossed a cow with a washing machine?

A milk shake!

★☽★

What did the wizard say about the stupid skeleton?

In one ear and out the other!

★★★

How did the wizard's dog put the movie on hold?

He hit the paws button!

★☽★

What did the wizard get when he crossed a lightbulb with his hometown?

Electri-city!

What kind of shoes do frogs wear?

Open-toad sandals!

★ ☾ ★

Why couldn't the ghost see the wizard?

He wasn't wearing his spooktacles!

★★★

Why did the wizard need a monitor for his pet?

Because it was a computer mouse!

★ ☾ ★

What did the ghost say to its wife?

Hello, boo-tiful!

Why was the wizard's frog so full and happy?

> *Because he ate everything that bugged him!*

★★★

What did the wizard get when he crossed a frog with a towel?

> *A rubbit!*

★☽★

What did the toads in the wizard's swamp eat when they wanted junk food?

> *French flies!*

★★★

What did the wizard get when he crossed an elephant and a butterfly?

> *A mam-moth!*

★☽★

Why do wizards wear pointy hats?

> *To keep their sharp minds warm!*

Jimmy: Are there any wizards who play basketball?

Timmy: Certainly!

Jimmy: Name one!

Timmy: *Magic Johnson!*

★ ☽ ★

"Knock, knock!"

"Who's there?"

"Ghoul!"

"Ghoul who?"

"Ghoul be sorry if you don't open up!"

What did the wizard say to the snake that bit him?

Fangs a lot!

★★★

Old wizard: Are you sure that your spell gave your mother eight legs?
Young wizard:

Sure, I'm sure. I just spider!

★☾★

How did the wizard get his car home after it broke down?

He toad it!

★★★

Why do witches come out only on Halloween?

Because they're crazy for candy!

★☾★

What was the ogre's favorite dish?

Ghoul-ash!

What did the wizard get when he combined a necklace with an alarm clock?

A diamond ring!

★ ☽ ★

What did the wizard think of the scary movie?

He thought it was dreadful!

★★★

What kind of movies do witches like best?

Hag-shun films!

What did the wizard say when he cast a sleeping spell on his cat?

Why don't you paws for a moment?

★★★

What did the toad say when the princess wouldn't kiss him?

Warts the matter with you?

★☽★

What did the wizard get when he crossed a python with a drinking cup?

A snake in the glass!

★★★

What did the wizard call the cow that went over the moon?

High jumper!

★☽★

What did the wizard call the horse's back?

A mane frame!

When the young wizard turned a dog into a frog, what did his father say?

What did I tell you about cursing in the house?

★☽★

What kind of nuts do frogs like?

Croak-o-nuts!

Where did the country wizard go to get supplies?

The farm-acy!

★★★

How did the wizard feel when a satellite fell into his yard?

Star struck!

★☽★

What do wizards put in potions to make people fat?

In-greed-ients!

★★★

What color was the wizard's cat?

Purr-ple!

★☽★

What do you call a wizard who loves telescopes?

Astrono-merlin!

What did the wizard say about the rowboat going around the moat?

Looks like it's in oar-bit!

★ ☾ ★

How did the star-happy wizard like to eat his cookies?

With a Milky Way!

★★★

What did the astronomer wizard sing in the bath?

"When You Wash Upon a Star"!

★ ☾ ★

What did wizard get when he stuck his nose in a jar?

Ring around the nosie!

★★★

What dish do goblins like best?

Mon-stir fry!

Why do wizards have stars and moons on their hats?

They need a little personal space!

★★★

What did the wizard tell the movie star?

I think you've got a fan-to-see!

★☽★

What did the wizard call the monster that ate its brother?

A munch-kin!

What did the wizard get when he crossed a snake and a king?

A king cobra!

★ ☽ ★

What did the wizard use to catch a fish for dinner?

Hali-bait!

★★★

What did the wizard call the twin ghosts?

A-pair-itions!

★ ☽ ★

What kind of car do creepy-crawly witches drive?

Beetles!

★★★

What did the wizard say to the witty ogre?

You've got a troll sense of humor, don't you?

What do you call witches who work in hospitals?

Health scare!

★★★

What did the wizard make his crazy friend for dessert?

Upside-down kook!

★ ☽ ★

What did the wizard call the knight with no home?

The Bedless horseman!

★☽★

What did the wizard call the little gourds that he had grown?

Pumpkin-bred!

★★★

What did the wizard get when he crossed a pumpkin with a plant?

Jack o' lan-fern!

★☽★

What did the wizard call the cloak that he had made out of fish?

A cape cod!

★★★

What did the wizard say about his wife's longest spell?

She was in a cast for weeks!

What do you call 12-dozen worms on a wizard's counter?

Gross!

★☽★

When do ghosts graduate?

When they have the fright stuff!

★★★

What did the wizard say when he saw a bull in the sky?

Must be a bull moon!

When did the dragon finally get full?

Around mid-knight!

★ ☽ ★

What do you call the wizard who is hungry for astronomy?

Star-ving!

★★★

What did the witch use as a spell to get jewelry?

Boil and bauble!

★ ☽ ★

Where did the wizard keep the power source for his basement?

In the dungeon-erator!

★★★

What did the wizard call the statues on his walls when the sun made them hot?

Gar-boils!

Where did the wizard keep the seeds for his garden?

Up in the flower tower!

★★★

What did the wizard say about the stupid monarch?

He ruled the whole king-dumb!

★☽★

What did the wizard call the young king who kept falling down?

Prince Harming!

★★★

What did the wizard call the king who wouldn't come down out of the tower?

His royal high-ness!

★☽★

What did the wizard call the king of the monsters in Scotland?

His Loch Ness Highness!

What did the wizard say when he had to sell one of his paintings?

It's only a poor-trait!

★★★

What did the wizard get when he crossed a skunk and a TV set?

Smell-o-vision!

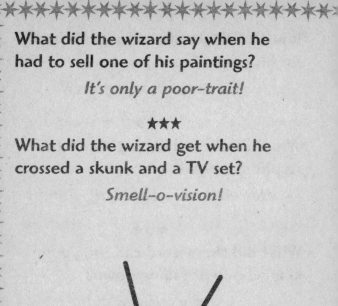

How did the monster scare the wizard?

He crypt up on him!

★ ☽ ★

Why did the wizard's butler wear a suit of armor?

Because he was a Sir-vant!

★ ☽ ★

Where did the wizard go to withdraw a crystal ball?

To a fortune teller!

★ ★ ★

What did the wizard call the psychic who kept growing?

Fortune Taller!

★ ☽ ★

What did the wizard call the monster named Theodore?

Demon Ted!

What did the rabbit say to the sorcerer?

Wiz up, doc?

★ ☽ ★

What did the wizard say after his wife starting throwing dishes?

Look out! Flying saucers!

★★★

What did the wizard get when he crossed a planet with a dish?

The World Cup!

★ ☽ ★

What do wizards like about alphabet soup?

They can spell while they eat!

★★★

What did the wizard call the knight's naughty horse?

A night mare!

What did the witch call the wizard
with no hair?

Baldy locks!

★☽★

What do you call a strange hairy wizard?

A beardo!

★★★

What did the wizard's wife say when
he bought her a new cloak?

Oh, you're so robe-mantic!

★☽★

What did the wizard call the jewelry
that he gave to his wife?

Married treasure!

★★★

What did the wizard call the scales
he dug up in the backyard?

Buried measure!

What did the wizard call the dog after he had shrunk it?

Spot!

★☾★

What did the wizard get when he crossed a bird and a writing tool?

A pen-guin!

**What did the wizard say when his pen
exploded?**

I've got that inking feeling again!

★ ☽ ★

How do you know if a wizard is happy?

He's going through a smiling spell!

★★★

**What did the wizard say about working
with animals?**

It's aard-vark!

★ ☽ ★

**What did the wizard get when he
crossed a potato with a priest?**

A chip-monk!

★★★

**What do wizards do before they
go to bed?**

They spell their prayers!

★ ☽ ★

What did the wizard call the necklace made out of lettuce?

Salad gold!

★★★

Where do wizards get their honey?

From spelling bees!

★☽★

What did the wizard call the resting place for birds?

Cemet-airy!

★★★

What did the wizard call his surly servant?

Stormy waiter!

★☽★

How do wizards remember?

They visit Memory Lane!

★★★

What instrument does a wizard on vacation play?

The Bermuda triangle!

★ ☾ ★

Which space-cadet singer do astronomer wizards like best?

Ricky Martian!

★★★

Which singing girls group do witches like best?

The Spice Ghouls!

★ ☾ ★

What did the wizard get when he crossed a movie star and a monster?

E-lizard Beth Taylor!

★★★

What did the wizard call the monster that wore a robe?

The Kimono Dragon!

Why did the monster's guitar sound so good after being in the basement for a long time?

Because it had been tombed!

★ ☽ ★

What did the wizard say about the shy witch?

Oh, she's just bats-full!

★★★

Why did the wizard love to tell jokes to his owl?

Because the owl always gave a hoot!

★ ☽ ★

What did the wizard call the Hobbit's hole?

Gnome's sweet home!

★★★

Why did the wizard's dog run so fast?

He was trying to cats-up!